B

House Beautiful

DETAILS

House Beautiful

DETAILS

The Editors of House Beautiful Magazine

Louis Oliver Gropp, Editor in Chief ～ Margaret Kennedy, Editor

Text by Sally Clark

HEARST BOOKS

NEW YORK

Library of Congress Cataloging-in-Publication Data

House beautiful details / the editors of House beautiful
magazine: Louis Oliver Gropp, editor in chief; Margaret Kennedy, editor; text by Sally Clark.
    p. cm.
Includes index.
ISBN 0-688-12588-3, 1-58816-014-9
1. Interior decoration accessories. I. Gropp, Louis Oliver. II. Kennedy, Margaret
(Margaret S.) III. House beautiful
IV. Title.
NK2115.5.A25C63   1996
747--dc20   95-41275
                                                              CIP

Printed in Singapore
First Edition
2 3 4 5 6 7 8 9 10

Edited by LAURIE ORSECK   Designed by NANCY STEINY DESIGN
Produced by SMALLWOOD & STEWART, INC., NEW YORK

www.housebeautiful.com

CONTENTS

FOREWORD BY LOUIS OLIVER GROPP • PAGE 10 ∾ INTRODUCTION • PAGE 12

CHAPTER 1
PORTRAITS IN STYLE • 15

CHAPTER 2
THE EDITING PROCESS • 33

CHAPTER 3
DRAWING ON COLOR • 53

CHAPTER 4
SURFACE STRATEGIES • 67

CHAPTER 5
PERSONAL EXPRESSION • 87

CHAPTER 6
THE COLLECTOR'S ART • 101

CHAPTER 7
FORCE OF NATURE • 117

CHAPTER 8
ELEMENTS OF SURPRISE • 129

DIRECTORY OF DESIGNERS AND ARCHITECTS • PAGE 140
PHOTOGRAPHY CREDITS • PAGE 143 ∾ ACKNOWLEDGMENTS • PAGE 144

FOREWORD

WHEN world-famous architect Mies van der Rohe said that "God is in the details," he was talking about buildings, but the same profound truth applies to the art of decoration as well. For that reason, I wasn't at all surprised to find the writer of this book, Sally Clark, beginning her introduction with the statement, "Details are the soul of decoration." That is the premise behind this volume, in which we document that it is the details of a room that give it personality, or "soul." Unfortunately, some rooms lack this quality altogether; even though they have perfectly fine furnishings, appropriately arranged, we find them simply unpublishable. On the other hand, there are rooms in which the personality of the owner is so revealed that it seems almost an intrusion to enter them with a camera. ☾ Sometimes when we love things too much, we lack the discipline to make choices, to exercise self-control. As the pages to follow illustrate, it is in editing the details of a room that the designer becomes an artist: making decisions about color, texture, and composition; arranging objects; taking risks; making a place one's own. God may be in the details, but you should be, too, if you want to create a room with soul.

Louis Oliver Gropp
EDITOR IN CHIEF

INTRODUCTION

DETAILS are the soul of decoration. A room may have superbly painted or papered walls and boast an arrangement of comfortable upholstery, but it is an unfinished shell until the paintings and prints, personal mementos, books, and lamps are in place. Stressing the importance of details in design, Billy Baldwin, the famous American decorator, observed that a room full of empty tables has "about as much charm as four blank walls." In his own Manhattan apartment, Baldwin painted the walls chocolate brown and chose brass lamps and étagères, a lacquered screen, and bibelots of wood and tortoiseshell. The room became famous and inspired a fashion for brown walls. The copycats missed the point, however. The chocolate-colored walls were not what made the apartment chic. The real source of stylishness was the details, and the flair the designer demonstrated in combining their various matte and glossy finishes. The brown backdrop was merely his canvas.

An enormous range of decorating items qualifies as accessories ~ paintings, photographs, prints, art glass, cachepots, pottery, sculpture, flowers. Area rugs, throw pillows, lamps and other light sources also warrant consideration as accents, for although they are functional design details, they make a strong esthetic contribution as well. Often, too, a piece of furniture can be thought of as an accent, especially when its design is highly unusual. Unique chairs, stools, ottomans, and other striking seating pieces definitely fall into this category.

Selecting and arranging finishing touches is the most rewarding aspect of decoration, for in the details lies the essence of a room's style and character. The pages that follow feature myriad ideas for organizing and displaying accents to create or complement a wide spectrum of decorating styles, as well as suggestions for using them to achieve the most dramatic results. Most of the rooms were designed by professionals, and their innovative approaches provide a wealth of inspired examples well worth adapting. Every aspect of this process is winningly illustrated in profiles of homes throughout the country, from a Santa Fe adobe retreat to a Federal house in Maine to a New York City apartment. By studying the vital part that details play in these interiors, you will discover truly imaginative ways to make accents powerful elements in the decoration of your own home.

CHAPTER I
PORTRAITS IN STYLE

IT IS NOT just a figure of speech to call accessories finishing touches. They are vital elements in decoration, the final strokes that give a room a polished, completed appearance. Without them, a decor would seem only partly done. But accessories and accents have a deeper meaning in interior design. They act like road signs, quickly transmitting the design direction that a room is taking. The profusion of objects chosen ~ or, by contrast, the very absence of them ~ provides additional messages about a decor. ℂ The interiors on the pages that follow reveal the various ways in which details can be used to enhance a broad spectrum of decorating styles, from traditional to modernist to contemporary. As different as these homes are from one another, in all of them the accents and accessories do share a common cause: Like hand-writing, they are telltale indicators of the tastes and personalities of the people who live in them.

BUILDING CHARACTER
IN A NEW HOUSE

THE YOUTHFULNESS of this recently built house is artfully disguised by the details with which the New Orleans design firm Holden & Dupuy dressed its rooms. By mixing antique furniture and accessories, both Continental and English, with unique and unusual handcrafted objects and accents, they turned the house's callow spaces into interiors of wordly wise sophistication and character.

Designed as a cool refuge against the subtropical Louisiana climate, the huge house has thick plaster walls, limestone floors, and 14-foot ceilings. As a contrast to these smooth, hard architectural surfaces, partners Ann Holden and Ann Dupuy used soft-to-the-touch, extremely luxurious fabrics through the house. Iridescent silk taffeta curtains puddle on the dining room floor; curtain panels of plush velvet, quilted in a diamond pattern to emphasize its rich pile, hang in the living room. Gauzy tissue silk slipcovers envelop spare dining room chairs, and silk plissé hangings adorn the canopy bed in the master bedroom. Cream damask ripples on cushiony armchairs, antique Italian settees boast lush velvet stripes.

Against these regal soft furnishings, the designers placed treasured antique objects, handpicked from all over the world, rich in history, and burnished by age. Rounded shapes predominate, making the rooms more inviting ("Curves are a lot more sensual and esthetically pleasing than straight angles," says Dupuy). An extraordinary eighteenth-century gilded sunburst mirror, discovered in London, embellishes the living room mantel. A gilded angel from a New York City dealer cavorts on a desk in the living room. A pair of cherub carvings ("Portuguese or Italian, and probably originally from a boat," says Dupuy) serves as the bases for side tables flanking the fireplace. And everything is overscale in keeping with the height of the ceilings.

On top of this decor, the designers added a layer of highly stylized and unusual handcrafted objects. They commissioned a New Orleans craftsman to fabricate a fireplace screen resembling a medieval triptych based on their own drawings. And after mulling over fabric possibilities for the decorative pillows destined for a raffia-wrapped sofa, the partners realized that only "one-of-a-kind things, pieces of art" would do. The Renaissance portrait pillows that resulted, from the workshop of a Louisiana artisan, are completely in keeping with an interior made unique by its finishing touches.

The screen in front of the fireplace is ornamented with glittering gold stars and crosses. Its curved shape allows the antique mantel to be seen but masks the gaping hole of the firebox. The antique cherub carving on the desk is nearly 3 feet tall.

To underscore the grandeur of the house, the designers chose both furniture and accessories with voluptuous forms. A pair of golden Italian sconces flank an eighteenth-century painted and gilded console, also Italian (opposite). Adding the playfulness of pattern is a leather throw rug handpainted with zebra stripes. To accessorize a raffia-covered settee of their own design (above left), Holden & Dupuy commissioned Louisiana artist Jacques Lamy to execute a pair of Renaissance-style portraits on artist's canvas and turn them into pillow artworks (below left). Cherubs cavorting in a French grisaille over the sofa continue the Renaissance theme.

CLASSICALLY MODERN

A CELEBRATION of twentieth-century modernism, this house outside Baltimore was designed in 1959 by famed Bauhaus architect Marcel Breuer for Edith Hooper, a great patron of modern art. The long, narrow house settles into the natural wooded landscape. Walls of rough Maryland stone dominate each room, and built-in bookshelves, credenzas, and cabinets keep furniture needs to a minimum.

Recently, the house was restored by New York architect Jonathan S. Foster. He kept the rooms exactly as Hooper had furnished them. In keeping with the spareness of modern design, the accent pieces are minimal, but in interiors so dedicated to a period, even the furniture can be considered a significant detail, and in this house almost every object is a twentieth-century classic: A Noguchi paper lamp casts light on an Alvar Aalto coffee table and a Le Corbusier tapestry in the family room. An Eero Saarinen coffee table in the living room sits opposite a Charles Eames lounge chair and ottoman of rosewood and black leather. Nearby is a Florence Knoll sofa, brightened by pillows of nubby woven textiles in orange and red.

The house, the furnishings, the accessories are all of a period. In faithfulness to classic twentieth-century design, down to the last small detail, the house Breuer created for Mrs. Hooper looks as fresh and bold now as when it was built more than 30 years ago.

In the family room, the architecture itself becomes the applied decoration. The fireplace was cast in concrete on the site, and the entire façade was bush-hammered to emphasize its rough texture. Other objects in the room display the same integrity of pure, unadorned material, including the glass and wood Alvar Aalto coffee table and the Noguchi lamp made of pleated rice paper. A simple clutch of tulips adds a spot of color; any more accessories would be superfluous.

Resting on the dining room credenza is a small Noguchi lamp and several Scandinavian modernist pieces, including silver and glass candlesticks from Georg Jensen (above).

The rollicking artwork displayed on the console and walls (opposite) are Henri Matisse's Jazz series prints; their bright colors seem to leap out from the neutral-toned stone wall.

EASTERN EXPOSURE

THE HORIZON line is definitely low in this apartment. Resting on tatami mats placed at precise angles on the floor are low tables, legless chairs, lacquered red boxes, and simple pottery bowls. All is tranquil and calm ~ until, perhaps, one happens to glance out the window and see not billboards in Japanese but the Empire State Building.

This studio apartment is in New York City, of course, but the esthetic is entirely Japanese. It is a serene world in which everything is arranged according to the venerable traditions of Eastern custom. With furniture and objects spare and close to the ground, the room seems enormous ~ one solution for coping with the constraints of a typically tiny Manhattan studio that must serve as living room, dining room, and bedroom.

When a decor concentrates so completely on a distinctive style as this one does, the smallest object borrowed from another design scheme would be a decorating faux pas, and immediately noticeable. But there is nothing jarring here. Hundreds of years of Japanese craft tradition stand behind many of the furnishings and accents. The pottery and lacquered tables have been handcrafted in the same simple shapes for generations. "The Japanese choose an object because it is pleasing to the eye or the touch," the owner explains.

In this authentically Asian landscape, Western bibelots are intruders. Neither a Chippendale chest nor a neon plastic storage cube belongs; instead, traditional Japanese pieces are put to untraditional uses or made to do double duty. Red lacquer boxes originally intended for serving slivers of raw fish are transformed into receptacles for checks and photographs. The decorative folding screen in the corner conceals the rolled-up futon and bedding that come out at night. An inlaid antique piece that is a stool by day becomes a bedside table. Not a single object is out of place in any sense.

In this Japanese interior in the heart of Manhattan, every object is decoratively authentic, from the bonsai plants to the handle-less cups on the table. Framed prints and photographs resting on the floor hold the site lines appropriately low. A vase of graceful, long-stemmed irises is in keeping with the stylized setting.

Antique Japanese wares are mixed with modern pieces throughout the apartment; many vintage objects were inherited from the owner's family. The folding screen anchoring one corner of the room (left) is a department store purchase made of handmade paper. Prints and wood-cuts, both old and new, are propped along the walls. Square lacquered boxes contain still-life arrangements of wave-tossed glass pieces and shells (above).

STANDING TRADITION
ON ITS HEAD

DESIGNER Gretchen Mann is mad for finials. Tall, skinny finials and short, twirly ones, bulbous wooden finials and tapered metal ones. Simple old American examples catch her attention; so do elaborately turned antique French versions shimmering with gold paint. For over a decade, the Connecticut decorator has pursued her quarry ~ architectural fragments long orphaned from the buildings they once embellished ~ in flea markets and junk shops throughout New England. The fruits of her efforts have resulted in an intriguing design symbiosis: The finials, no matter how lowly their origin, seem to be transformed once Mann gets them back to her airy Victorian house, and they, in turn, give her otherwise traditional rooms an offbeat and highly personalized flavor.

The two criteria that guide Mann in her continuous search are shape ~ anything from smooth spheres to carved pineapples to spinning tops ~ and finish ("If it has the original old wiped-off paint finish, that's a good sign of age," she explains). To make the contoured forms stand out, she sets the finials against walls and furnishings held to a strict palette of black, beige, white, and gray. In such neutral surroundings, the reclaimed architectural cast-offs are born again as unique and fascinating ornaments. The designer arranges them with the ceremony and care that others devote to Ming porcelains. She clusters them on tables and groups them on chests, placing them so the varying sizes and shapes play off one another. A room with traditional bricabrac can appear stiff, but Mann's architectural objects are a wry decorative icebreaker. Their presence relaxes her American and European antique furniture and adds a zing of originality to her rooms.

The worn, peeled-paint finish of a pair of French finials on Mann's living room mantel is a perfect foil to the room's classic furnishings. Several more finials from her large collection are artfully crowded on a side table. Instead of the staid family portrait that was customarily hung over parlor mantels in New England, the designer delivered her witty punchline: a giant watch, a trade sign relic from an old London jewelry shop.

In the master bedroom (left), the top of an American primitive cupboard serves as an exhibit space for a quartet of finials with eccentric shapes. The vintage barometer, a veritable sunburst of arrows, offsets the solidness of the finials and keeps the arrangement from being too weighty. In another bedroom (above), Mann placed a huge bouquet of country flowers in a nineteenth-century urn, which rests on a platform of black terra-cotta blocks that she commissioned for just that purpose. Similar urns are used through the house.

CHAPTER 2

THE EDITING PROCESS

THE SHEER number of accents and accessories that are placed in any given room depends to a large degree on the basic style of that room. A sleek, minimal contemporary scheme will not remain so if it becomes too loaded with objects. A profusion of items, however ~ even clutter ~ may actually enhance an English country setting and make it cozier and more charming. For people like Manhattan designer Michael de Santis, a few details are enough. "I like them," he explains, "but if you have too many you don't see them." For those who consider empty spaces blank spaces, though, plenty of details are an absolute requirement, providing a much-needed visual feast. Such people undoubtedly subscribe to the antique dealers' adage that a pair of anything is better than one, and a collection is preferable to two. In the end, however, there are no absolute answers. When it comes to these elements of design, beauty is indeed in the eye of the editor.

FIVE GUIDING LIGHTS

EVEN THE most talented designer will admit that arranging accessories successfully is a process of trial and error; it may take several tries with various objects before a grouping really works.

Helping navigate the editing process are five esthetic guidelines: color, shape, scale, texture, and finish. Using them as reference points, a designer begins by looking for similarities as well as contrasts among objects. Two pieces with different bold shapes ~ one curved, one angular ~ may set up an exciting contrast. Or the repetition of the same shape, as in a collection of plates on a wall, may achieve the desired effect. In a room where ceilings soar and the furniture is imposing, details should be appropriately overscale. Disparate objects drawn from different periods, places, and pedigrees can mesh successfully when all share similar colors, finishes, and textures. This is a useful trick when operating on a tight budget: One or two precious items can be augmented with finds from thrift shops and flea markets that are in some ways similar.

But sometimes only an adventurous approach will do. In an arrangement of boxes, for example, a striking visual statement might be created by grouping unlike surfaces and colors together ~ a dark, polished mahogany tea caddy and a carved walnut case with a worn, dull finish can be surprisingly and successfully teamed with a pair of red lacquered oriental boxes.

A few carefully chosen framed photographs, all on deep white mattings, are set out in pairs beneath and on top of a desk. The arrangement sets up a pleasant repetition of angular forms and mitigates the plainness of the furniture. A giant portrait against the wall provides an exciting contrast.

Designer Frank Babb Randolph likes his rooms unfussy and spare, a preference that is evident in the details of his Washington, D.C., townhouse. In the living room, three simple accessories ~ a vase of flowers, an antique terracotta vessel, and a starfish ~ find a place on the shagreen coffee table (opposite).

A contemporary painting hangs over the fireplace; as a contrast to the painting's smooth sepia field of color, the designer banked the mantel in the rough textures of dried leaves and branches. ℂ "Simple, functional, nice to look at, and inexpensive" is how magazine stylist Jane Cumberbatch describes her decorating taste. The

mantel garniture in the sitting room of her 1726 London house bears out her description (above). Using ordinary objects at hand, she placed six plain clay flowerpots in graduated sizes at regular intervals along the marble shelf. The repeated shapes and the contrast in the pots' sizes make the grouping intriguing.

On a Federal mantel, designer Jeffrey Bilhuber set out a trio of modern prints and drawings, an ornate eighteenth-century candlestick, and a primitive artifact (left). The individual pieces are exquisite and compelling, but it is their dissimilarity ~ of shape, material, and cultural origins ~ that creates visual tension and holds the viewer's gaze. ☾ A shock of orange-red tulips plays off the stark black and white photo-graph in the foyer of Steven Charlton and Jeffrey Goodman's home (above). A metal vase with a dull finish acts as a counterpoint to the shiny gold-toned frame.

In order to keep
attention focused on its
magnificent Georgian
revival woodwork,
stylist Tricia Foley
used a light touch in
arranging the mantel in
her 1870s Manhattan
townhouse (above).
An old clock in the center
is surrounded by an
equal number of ivory
candles and vases
bursting with ivory roses
on either side. ❡ In a
modern adaptation of
an early-nineteenth-
century Regency room by
Irvine & Fleming
(opposite), designer Sam
Blount arranged
fine toleware, prints,
and porcelains to create
the impression of
objects that had been
collected over time.
A mantel filled with bits
of family history ~
photographs, invitations,
and postcards tucked
into an antique mirror ~
lends the room a
decidedly intimate air.

The profusion of details in Barrie McIntyre's library in Kent, England, creates a haven that is warm, handsome, and the essence of English country house style (opposite). Planning and organization keep the quantity of objects in the room from being overwhelming. A sizable collection of historic copper-plate prints, all matted and framed alike, is displayed in large symmetrical groups that anchor the room and give a sense of stability to the array of smaller objects all around. Needlepoint pillows the color of cloisonné enamel provide a counterpoint to the polished wood furniture and picture frames. On a table near the door, the statuary fragment of a woman's head is offset by smaller treasures ~ marble spheres on one side, a statue's lost hand on the other (above).

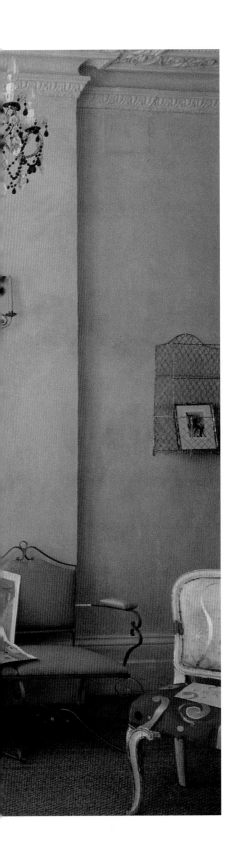

The antique curtsies to the avant-garde in London designer Carolyn Quartermaine's studio (left). Dressed in collages fashioned from scraps of the calligraphy fabrics Quartermaine designs, old French chairs take a bow as one-of-a-kind accents. On largely unadorned chalky pink walls, delicate gold sconces sparkle like jewels on the ears of a Victorian belle. ❦ On antiques dealer Corey Daniels' parlor mantel (above), a quaint portrait of a young girl and a carefully chosen and arranged medley of white objects ~ a china server, eggshells, and flowers ~ creates a spirited play of light and dark.

No ordinary wall shelf would do in designer Mariette Himes Gomez's apartment (left). Always innovative in her design decisions, she chose an architectural fragment with an interesting shape and transformed it into a striking yet functional piece. The carefully edited display includes a lilliputian chest and a golden vase. ☾ Four objects come together to shake up this cream white room by designer Jorge Letelier and create a provocative tableau (opposite). The Native American rugs and portrait share a common palette of red, brown, and ivory. Throwing a bold curve is a chair by English designer Tom Dixon, so lively it almost prances.

AN ARTFUL ARRANGER
PRACTICES HIS CRAFT

MANY OF THE compositions that Corey Daniels creates with his antiques are vivid examples of how expert editing becomes art. Daniels, an antiques dealer in Maine, studied to be an artist at the Boston Museum School. "For me," he says, "decorating is like making a painting or sculpture." His montages reveal the concern for color, shape, scale, texture, and finish that are the decorator's hallmarks, and the esthetic principles he absorbed as a student are always tugging at his elbow.

Daniels is blessed with a true dealer's eye for the character and romance of an object. For years he specialized in Early American antiques, but these days he finds himself equally drawn to European pieces. He has a taste for the common as well as the rare, the ordinary as well as the extraordinary, and he is as likely to amass well-worn flea market trifles as he is to seize on fine paintings and sculpture. Architectural fragments, frames, bits of coral and shell, pewter, carved and turned wood finials, busts, and old paintings are his particular passions. Old painted surfaces beckon him; his antique painted chests and consoles are time-worn and sun-faded; his collection of vintage frames and whittled woodwork is flaking with paint and gilding.

When it came to furnishing the fifteen rooms in his eighteenth-century house, he indulged himself by putting all the pieces together in one delightful magpie exhibition. Good American pewter plates share shelf space with English Victorian majolica, French creamware, and Continental silver. Tabletops are laden with ironstone pitchers, Native American baskets, and finials of every stripe. Interspersed throughout are the natural objects Daniels loves for their creamy tones ~ seashells, white coral, ocean-smoothed sea stones. The groupings, highly personal works of art brokered by the collector's sense of playfulness and wit, keep all fifteen rooms endlessly fascinating.

A gilded nineteenth-century wood frame, long separated from its painting, shares a console with an Italian Baroque finial spouting golden flames (opposite). The pairing works because of the worn painted finishes the objects have in common, and because of the shapes they do not. An English Regency sewing box and a burnished metal Persian-made antelope round out the tableau.

Small antiques on an
eighteenth-century
painted French chest are
a study in curves
and contours (right).
Beneath an 1840s
American clock, Daniels
placed a white marble
bust, a fancy finial, and
an alabaster urn.
Granite balls are jumbled
in a metal basket.
On a kitchen shelf, the
curved edge of an
old metal tray forms an
appealing backdrop
for a montage of every-
day objects (above).

CHAPTER 3

DRAWING ON COLOR

COLOR is the most immediate of an object's properties. It is also the most emotional, capable of imbuing a pillow, a chair, or any other detail with enough energy to affect the spirit of the setting and the mood of the beholder. Changing the color of accessories, then, can make a dramatic statement in a room. Against glazed lemon-yellow walls, an assortment of brilliant Matisse prints, jewel-toned pillows, and vibrant art glass is energizing and exciting. But replacing these bright treasures with cream-colored damask pillows, vintage black and white etchings, and a group of creamware pitchers immediately quiets down the room and gives it a more serene quality. ℂ Introducing color through pattern can stir up a design scheme and make it livelier. The field of the pattern may be small, as on an Imari bowl, or expansive, as in a wall-size tapestry. The art of combining solid and patterned colors gives a room both character and depth.

TONES OF VOICE

IN THE WORLD of details, there are a number of time-honored ways to use color to its best advantage. Many people choose neutral settings and accessories for their soothing qualities; to prevent such decorating schemes from appearing bland and unfinished, however, the accents chosen should represent a range of values. (Value refers to the lightness or darkness of a color.) In a room with cream-colored walls, for example, ebony picture frames, polished mahogany antique boxes, and tobacco-colored pillows will add resonance, especially if the furniture and carpet are paler neutrals.

But if the goal is to make that same cream-colored room appear vibrant, using bright colors is the solution: Imagine sofa pillows of saturated red and cadet blue, and posters drenched in hues pulled from a crayon box. (Accents in pastel tones will have an entirely different effect.)

The color of the background against which an object appears must also be taken into account. White walls often make the best backdrop, but various hues can display accents and objects just as radiantly, and sometimes more dramatically. Designer Mario Buatta never chooses white to show off fine paintings or antiques, opting instead for such distinctive tones as eggplant, emerald green, brilliant red, and lemon yellow.

While the treatments of large surfaces ~ the curtains, wallpaper, upholstery fabric ~ generally provide most of the pattern in a room, accessories can make a surprisingly effective contribution as well. Throw pillows, china and porcelains, and especially area rugs are all sources of pattern that can make a significant impact in a room. Placed strategically and used adventurously, they add sharpness and dimension. The more daring the mix, the richer the result.

Designer Michael Stanley painted the kitchen of his Connecticut house a creamy white to create an effective backdrop for his large collection of majolica pottery. He concentrated the pieces with leaf shapes in a single hutch, where their mottled green and brown glazed surfaces look lustrous in the light from a nearby window. The fruit-patterned fabric on the chair picks up the green tone and nature theme of the pottery.

The sitting room of
Boston framer and art
collector Roger Lussier
shimmers with the
luminosity of a Turner
painting. The space
is a subtle composition of
soft neutral-colored
accents against walls of
pearl gray ~ "I'm not
fond of most colors,"
Lussier says. "I'm very
happy with browns,
grays, creams, and
whites." Glints of gold
from antique armchairs,
a pair of candlestick
lamps, and a profusion
of gilded frames on
all the walls infuse the
serene setting with
energy and excitement.

The large-patterned wallpaper in Michael Stanley's dining room might have been too busy for the space, but by arranging milk glass plates on the walls, he tamed the pattern and kept its background from being cloying (opposite). The ruby glass on the table echoes the paper's juicy red berry color. ☾ To add flair to the tongue and groove paneling in her bathroom (above), Lady Jane Churchill grouped several blue and white plates on the wall above the tub. In the carefully thought-out display, two pairs of matching plates flank the one in the center.

Color glows from the glass, textiles, and other handcrafted details in the Manhattan apartment of Susie Elson, former chairwoman of the American Crafts Council, and her husband, Edward Elliott Elson, the United States ambassador to Denmark, two passionate collectors of contemporary crafts. In the dining room, where the details are the sole source of color, glass and ceramic works of art pose confidently on the table and on clear lucite shelving, which allows each piece to show through in all its intensity.

SPICING UP A FAMILY ROOM

WHEN HE WAS commissioned to create a family room with the emphasis on warmth and hospitality, New York designer Charles Morris Mount turned to a high-spirited mix of color and pattern to achieve his aim. He and colleague Kelly Greeson envisioned a space that would be in direct contrast to the sleekness and seriousness of the adjacent kitchen, an expanse of white counters and cabinets edged with crisp black accents.

Their first step was to add a fireplace with a large raised hearth, tall windows on either side, and skylights piercing the ceiling. Then they painted the walls a frosty white. In this space, light and airy as an art gallery, they mobilized the forces of color. A tomato-red sofa sits in front of the hearth, and on each side of it is a well-padded contemporary armchair upholstered in a two-tone combination of putty and marine blue. Accents are placed decisively: orange roll-shaped pillows on the armchairs, and a plump throw pillow in marine blue on the sofa. A large and colorful collage fills one wall. A kilim area rug, in a strong pattern of offbeat teal and pinky-terra-cotta hues on a cocoa ground, animates the center of the room. As a final flourish of riotous pattern and color, a black and orange quilt exploding with starbursts serves as a tablecloth. The result is a down-to-earth, comfortable, lighthearted spot for reading, relaxing, and enjoying meals.

Brown accents ~ camel-toned pillows and a soft chocolate-colored chenille throw ~ are inviting details on a bright red sofa in this family room. The cocoa-colored background of the kilim rug underfoot extends the brown accents throughout the room. The designers chose a coffee table with a clear glass top to let all the colors show through.

The color scheme in the family room is mirrored in a large wall collage (left). Pillows in orange and blue set off the boldly shaped and colored upholstery, while touches of cool blue cut the room's predominant hot and spicy curry tones. On the dining room table (above), the golden sunbursts of the quilt-cum-tablecloth reiterate the warm tones of the rattan chairs. The cerulean sky in the barnyard painting offers another refreshing chromatic pause.

CHAPTER 4
SURFACE STRATEGIES

THE ARCHITECTURAL surfaces of a room ~ walls, floors, ceilings ~ are often taken quite for granted, but they are major stages on which accents and accessories play their role in design. Walls, of course, are the prime architectural backdrop for a host of details ~ prints, paintings, photographs, tapestries, decorative sconces. Second in importance is furniture, which provides many flat surfaces for the placement of accents. Coffee tables, consoles, side tables, desks, hutches, secretaries, and bookcases are all potential staging areas. ℂ In selecting an appropriate spot for displaying an accessory, consideration must be given not only to the location of the surface, but to its texture, color, and sometimes pattern as well. The more attention lavished on the surface ~ a superior paint job on the wall, for example, or a fine polish on a mahogany coffee table ~ the more handsome the accents placed on it will appear. Surfaces may be backgrounds to details, but they never take a backseat.

GROUP THERAPY

IDEALLY the arrangement of objects in a room should create a series of "pausing points" that draw the viewer in. Sometimes the objects themselves are so strong and bold that they can perform on their own in achieving this end. A single large marble bust or ceramic vase may be enough to carry a coffee table. And in rooms that are intentionally spare, displaying single pieces in strategically chosen spots around the room enhances the clean lines of the decor.

More often, however, a group of objects will have greater impact than a single piece. But if it is not well balanced, the arrangement, regardless of the beauty or fineness of the objects involved, will not be pleasing to look at. Symmetry is the most obvious way to achieve this balance. A pair of tall candlesticks on a mantel, one at each end, is a familiar example. Less frequently seen, and therefore more intriguing, are arrangements that depend on asymmetry to create a sense of balance. Consider the same pair of candlesticks placed side by side on the mantel, with the rest of the mantel left bare; a painting hangs on the wall above the part of the bare shelf rather than in the usual centered position.

Variety ~ whether of objects or their placement ~ is another element

A variety of sizes makes a lineup of portraits far more interesting than would be true if they were all the same. Designer Peter Wheeler removed the paintings from their stretchers and tacked them directly to the wall. He propped a contemporary print on the right side of the bench below, then balanced off the arrangement by resting another print on the floor to the left.

that animates an arrangement. In a grouping of paintings and prints, displaying frames in several different shapes and sizes is more interesting than a wall paved with identical rectangles. Groupings of similar objects in a hutch can be enlivened by the addition of just one or two different ones ~ a bouquet of yellow tulips in a parade of blue and white Canton chargers and tureens, for example. Variety also adds animation to tablescapes, the term sometimes used to describe the arrangement of objects on tables and other flat surfaces. The most fascinating of these groupings invariably include contrasts of finish, color, texture, shape, and scale among the items included. A shiny brass candlestick works well against the dull leather bindings of a small antique book; the rough, rhythmic textures of a tramp art box provide a nice contrast to a smooth tole urn. Sumptuous live hydrangeas play handsomely against gnarled curly willow.

When it comes to wall arrangements, planning in advance is crucial. Before bringing out the hammer, it is helpful to sketch a grouping out on paper, especially if several sizes of pictures are to be used. Some designers suggest laying the pictures on the floor and working out the composition there.

A mirror placed low on a wall brings a potentially dead corner to life (opposite). Borrowing shapes from the mirror's ornate filigree frame, the chaise is covered in an arabesque-patterned damask, and the window treatments are edged in an intertwined geometric border as well. ❦ A fine Art Deco buffet acts as the stage for an arrangement of contemporary pottery (right). The pieces are grouped in two clusters ~ white ones to the left, colored ones to the right. The pair of Andy Warhol silkscreen portraits over them on the wall unifies the vignette.

An old Chinese folding screen, pressed into service as a wall hanging, becomes the focal point in designer Libby Cameron's living room (far left). Boldly patterned pillows on the sofa and a lively striped rug spike the traditional scheme. ☙ When several small paintings are tightly grouped together, as is this trio in designer Charles Spada's weekend house (above left), they read as a strong statement. ☙ Large canvases should be allowed to realize their full power. In designer Craig Raywood's Manhattan apartment, two huge paintings fill the walls of the living room (below left). Faux tortoise trim at ceiling height unifies and frames them.

On a highly polished mahogany table, design partners Joseph Lembo and Laura Bohn propped a small, ornately framed mirror in front of a large mahogany-edged looking glass, then introduced a decorative box in a contrasting shape (right). When a lamp is switched on nearby, the reflections from the various surfaces create a magical play of light and shadow. ❦ Robert K. Lewis started with an unusual gold mirror for an arrangement on a dining room wall (below right). He added framed antique seals above it and newly purchased platters on each side of it. A vintage cream-colored Wedgwood plate between the framed seals ties the vignette together. The coffeepot is a fine example of 1880s American silverplate.

Designer Katie Ridder
and her husband,
architect Peter Pennoyer,
have turned virtually
every surface of
their apartment into a
staging area for
their many collections.
On a fabric-covered
console (right), small
wooden boxes,
Middle Eastern urns,
and a painted ceramic
plate join forces.
The feathery topiaries
add a contrasting
note of greenery. On a
classic Biedermeier
table (below right), they
banked objects near
the wall, leaving the
main part of the
table clear for writing
letters. The collection of
treasures includes
simple geometric shapes ~
a marble pyramid
and a sphere ~ as well
as leather-bound
books and a miniature
gallery of prints
and photographs, all
to entertain the eye.

The most straightforward presentation brings out the best in country objects. Designers Lawrence Paolantonio and Pamela Gaylin Ryder devised a lineup of rough-textured pots on a robust sideboard for a pleasing display that spills on to the floor (opposite). The colors of the fruit in the wicker basket echo those in the painting above it, and the straw hats make a casual country gesture. ℂ On a simple pine writing table, a galvanized metal pail takes a star turn as a vase (above). Stylist Jane Cumberbatch used the pail's towering height as a contrast to the low horizon of the other objects on the table. The long-stemmed alliums playfully underscore the exaggeration of scale as well.

When groups of prints, photographs, or paintings are hung together, the space between each frame becomes a detail itself. Manhattan designer Eve Robinson left a good deal of room between three photographs of the Brooklyn Bridge, which added to the stature of each image (above).

❧ In designer Christian Liaigre's Paris living room (opposite), alternating narrow and wide spaces between four antique photographs sets up a pattern almost as pleasing as the pictures themselves.

A fireplace mantel provides rich opportunities for displaying mirrors, vases, bibelots, and art. In a modestly decorated room (left), the owner took a fresh, innovative approach to symmetry by balancing unlike objects ~ stacked boxes with a bowl of fruit, a tiny portrait with a vase of flowers ~ on the mantel. ☾ In striking contrast, a glamorous mantel decorated by Mario Buatta is crowned by an ornately gilded mirror that fills the entire fireplace wall (opposite). Shelves on either side house displays of daintily painted porcelains.

COVERING ALL THE BASES

DESIGNER Jeffrey Bilhuber is a self-confessed perfectionist who admits that he can "happily manipulate six objects on a table-top for four hours straight." He has had ample opportunity to do so in the last several years as he worked on the decor of an eighteenth-century Pennsylvania farmhouse. The owners had no desire to turn the refined old farmstead into a pseudo-English home fluffed with yards of floral chintz. Bilhuber, who loves to mix contemporary furniture with fine antique case pieces and clean-lined bookcases, antique bibelots, and contemporary art, was the perfect choice to take on the task of reviving the farmhouse.

Mindful of his clients' desire for comfort, Bilhuber judiciously kept table surfaces largely free of ornamentation. He took a spare approach to the walls as well, limiting the pictures in each room to a single theme ~ tulips in the dining room, pinecones in the library, wax seals in the living room. Then he created special painted backgrounds for each grouping to keep the single-theme tactic from becoming monotonous. In the living room, he used bold graphics for the punch of pattern and contrast. Broad stripes of cream and beige animate the walls. Batik throw pillows sit side by side with multileaf patterns and trellis checks on the chairs and sofas. Rough textures ~ nubby rugs, large pottery vessels, small sculptures poised on tables and chests ~ keep the rooms from being too formal.

In the living room, a collection of red antique seals is flanked by a pair of contemporary prints (opposite). The scarlet seals inspired the narrow border ~ less than an inch ~ of red striped wallpaper that outlines the entire room. ☾ Against offbeat yellow-green dining room walls, artist Rory McEwen's quartet of giant tulips is saved from sweetness (above).

The tablescape in the entryway is a casual grouping of contrasting textures and finishes. Earthenware vessels on the floor echo the shape of the console lamp; the pattern and colors of the area rug repeat the wall tones. All of the hallway's accessories stand out readily against the white chevron-paneled door and walls painted the juicy color of a ruby-red grapefruit.

*Worldly eclecticism
defines the choice
of details in the living
room. The burnished
colors of an antique
European tapestry are
counterbalanced by
the crisp graphics of the
pillows and wool
throw on the sofa. Well-
proportioned pieces of
sculpture in eye-catching
shapes and a wall
sconce in the shape of
a trio of trumpets
add interest to the room
without taking over.*

CHAPTER 5
PERSONAL EXPRESSION

EVERY ITEM with which we choose to live expresses our tastes and interests, even our professional lives. The photographs of childhood summers, of old college friends, of family celebrations that we tuck in a dresser mirror are intriguing intimate keepsakes; the collections of Victorian enamel boxes and art glass passed down from family members are small pieces of personal history. But what about the brushes and perfume bottles on the dresser, the pens and folders on a writing table, the books on a nightstand, the paint-brushes on the worktable, or the computer on the desk? Essential details in our lives, these practical objects can be appealing and important accents in our rooms as well. Indeed, the process of selecting and arranging the various pieces of our personal lives is as revealing as the souvenir snapshot of a cherished holiday. Assembled in a harmonious display, they form a captivating decorative album of our lives.

ELEVATING THE EVERYDAY

ARRANGING everyday objects in an attractive manner can present a decorating dilemma. Most of us are too busy ~ and too practical ~ to live the existence of the dedicated esthete. The sensitive creature who wraps the telephone directory in marbled papers to camouflage its commercial dreariness dwells in the pages of romance novels, not in the house next door. But no one wishes to be sloppy with the details of life, either. To renowned decorator Dorothy Draper, accessories were serious business. In speaking of an acquaintance who was negligent on that score, Draper spared no mercy. "One of the smartest women I know has a dowdy house," she wrote. "Her living room is ruined by fussy, old-fashioned lampshades; careless, mismatched fire tools; and a litter of unattractive knickknacks on all the small tables. . . . There is no use going into any more details. They are details ~ but so unbelievably important." The point the designer was making, of course, is that everything visible in a room is a decorative element, as much of an accent as a painting or a vase, and is not to be taken for granted. Everything from waste baskets and tissue boxes to the tools of one's trade ~ the artist's easel, the designer's drafting board, the computer ~ can be thought to serve a decorative purpose. That does not mean, however, that it is necessary to rush out to buy an antique set of fireplace tools or an expensive doodad to serve up paperclips. Functional everyday items do not have to be expensive or even unusual in their design. Simplicity often suffices. When the smallest details, from family photographs to home office supplies, are carefully arranged and pleasingly presented, the cumulative effect cannot help but make a room more inviting.

On a writing table, an array of interesting boxes used to keep home office paraphernalia neat presents an arresting still life; even the waste basket is smart looking. Operating on the theory that old wood looks good against yellow paint, Robert K. Lewis dressed the bisque-colored desk with a mahogany tea caddy to hold stamps and stashed stationery in an oak letter holder. For punch, he hung a striking contemporary collage on the wall.

Books, with their colorful covers and bindings, always warm up a room. On a long wall of glass shelves in this Manhattan apartment, journals, books, magazines ~ even a collection of compact discs ~ are gathered in small groups; displaying some of the stacks vertically and others horizontally adds visual interest. Punctuating the arrangement are framed photographs, personal mementos, and antique finds such as an old camera case and a wooden model of a ship hull. Nothing on the shelves is expensive, yet the overall display is strikingly handsome and highly personal.

Home furnishings stylist Ellen O'Neill has a flair for turning the least likely items to decorative use. In her own apartment, she piled the top of an old cupboard with vintage cigar and cigarette boxes (left). The boxes serve as hiding places for her hair accessories; the repetition of the labels creates a colorful little display. The amusing winged threadspool on the wall is a sign from a shop O'Neill once owned. On her bedroom dresser (opposite), O'Neill leaves her scarves and hats out in full view, providing spots of decorative color and pattern.

The drawings and models that Steven Charlton and Jeffrey Goodman produce for the furniture they design often become witty artwork for their Hollywood, California, home. Their droll Crawford chair is immortalized in a parade of framed watercolors (opposite) and a row of silvery miniature sculptures over the kitchen range (above left). Renderings of other designs and works-in-progress form a small gallery above a desk (below left).

WORKING OUT THE FINE POINTS

IN THE HUGE one-room atelier that Boston artist Ken Kelleher calls home, the objects of his trade are always on view. He makes no attempt to hide them, either. Instead, he treats his brushes and containers of paint as decorative details in their own right, arranging them in orderly groups on shelves and worktables all throughout the studio. What keeps it all from seeming like so much clutter is that most of the shelves, window ledges, tables, and containers in the room are a creamy white color. The brackets that support the shelves of paint cans are white; hammers and screwdrivers hang on a clean white pegboard; and the paint-brushes, which all seem to have pale wood handles, are arranged in cream-colored ceramic vases and jars. In this pale environment, the work tools blend so well with the surroundings that it takes a moment to be aware of them.

The extensive use of subdued tones in this space is a double-edged device. Not only are everyday objects cleverly camouflaged, but the peaceful monochromatic scheme creates a sense of serenity ideal for an artist. "Soft colors are soothing to have around," says Kelleher.

But in this studio, personal expression works on another level as well. The space doubles as a showplace for the unusual accents that Kelleher creates from the architectural fragments that he collects. He routinely scours Boston's antiques shops and haunts area flea markets in search of these fragments, along with small carvings and assorted vintage bits and pieces of every description, to turn into decorative objects. The elegant cream-colored table in his foyer sporting a medallion of the poet Petrarch is his creation; so, too, is the living room console with its robust curved supports. "It's all sheer fantasy," says Kelleher. He was speaking of one of his pieces, but he might just as well have been describing the wonderful assemblage of created objects and everyday details that fill his white-on-white studio home.

Found objects become art and carved fragments become unique furniture in the atelier home of Boston painter Ken Kelleher. To enshrine a carved medallion of the Italian poet Petrarch, the artist crafted a slender table for his entry. The overscale vase is a Victorian funerary urn, which was used to hold flowers at graveside.

Kelleher's two favorite pastimes ~ haunting New England's antiques markets and "fussing with my apartment" ~ happily feed each other. He turned discarded woodwork into Baroque-style supports for a marble top (left), then hung an Italian gilded mirror ~ an authentic treasure ~ above it. Another Kelleher concoction, a table with a lacy Gothic apron (below left), holds some of the artist's tools; others, set out on shelves and pegboards, are reflected in the mirror above it.

*Kelleher fashioned
an armillary sphere ~
an old astronomical
instrument ~ from wood
hoops salvaged from
an old drum (left). He
used a metal found
object to make the arrow,
then created the
golden orb in the center
from a croquet ball.
On his desk (below left),
amid books and
pencils, is a collection
of the diminutive,
beautifully shaped
sculptural pieces he loves,
including a tiny hand
and a dainty bust,
all sharing the same worn
black finish.*

CHAPTER 6

THE COLLECTOR'S ART

A WALL of beautifully framed sporting prints, a hutch filled with English Arts and Crafts metalwork, lucite shelves holding contemporary glass, tabletops filled with seashells ~ collections add immeasurable character to a room. Regardless of what we collect, however, there must be as much art to the display as in the objects themselves. Even if the collection is not inherently expensive or rare, a clever arrangement can create great impact, and often can camouflage shortcomings in the individual pieces. In a grouping of majolica pitchers, for example, every single one may not be unusual or in perfect condition, but the overall impression made by their blue-green colors and lustrous glazed surfaces is guaranteed to be powerful. When the objects in a collection are valuable and in perfect condition, a strong display is still important; even the most exceptional objects will be diminished by a sloppy or matter-of-fact presentation.

DISPLAY'S THE THING

FLEA MARKET finds and garage sale discoveries can look like glittering prizes when they are exhibited with flair. Consider, first, that a lot of anything is always interesting to look at ~ especially when the individual items are everyday objects. One old ceramic bowl may be just an odd piece of kitchenware, but six white ceramic bowls are a collection. The repetition of an object's properties ~ especially shape or color ~ creates drama and visual interest. That is what makes a few shelves of Fiestaware or old tin spatterware look as rich as choice antique pottery.

In a similar fashion, expert framing and arranging can turn ordinary objects ~ magazine covers, pages from old calendars, even vintage textiles ~ into decorative collections. When a city library cleared out volumes of children's picture books from the 1940s and 1950s, one clever mother bought several and snipped out the colorful drawings. She had them all framed alike, then hung them in her daughter's room, with charming results. Another woman, rather than use the 1940s fruit-printed dish towels she found at a tag sale, had three of them framed to hang on the kitchen wall. Still another created a unique foyer decoration by framing exquisite ladies' gloves ~ embroidered

Dalmatian spots, squiggles, ripples, and other blue and white patterns are shown to advantage when a collection of prize American spongeware is displayed on country shelves. The repetition of similar shapes, patterns, and colors makes the grouping an especially arresting one.

Victorian styles and 1950s couture creations ~ and hanging the frames at eye level.

If the objects are fine, a small number of them can more successfully stand on their own ~ a pair of exceptional French Art Deco silver candlesticks may be all the ornamentation a mantel needs. In fact, the more beautiful and rare the object, the less it needs around it.

The background against which objects are viewed is as important as the number of pieces displayed. Many collectors prefer white, cream, or beige walls, because these neutral colors allow the pieces themselves to dominate. But sometimes a colored background brings out the best in pieces of art, especially paintings, porcelains, and tapestries that are all from a single school or period and share a particular family of colors. Many modern canvases are hung against bold-colored walls, which add to the sumptuousness of the paintings. Yellow is often the background choice for collectors of Impressionist works, who find the color complements the sunny tones in their canvases. And fabric designer Manuel Canovas considers it the ideal background for the gilded frames and blue-gray matting of his antique prints. Experimenting with paint colors, as well as with shiny and dull finishes, is advisable.

Everyday objects can be as eye-catching as precious ones when they are arranged in an appealing way. In the mudroom of an eighteenth-century New England house refurbished by John Saladino, a parade of hats over the doorway is a charming addition (opposite). ℭ Ready to be grabbed for a country ramble, vintage walking sticks and umbrellas rest in an old metal stand at the Connecticut house of designer Charles Spada (above).

Pictures can be presented effectively in any size space; the success of a display depends on an interesting arrangement of frame shapes, sizes, and finishes. In a drawing room covered in brilliant yellow moiré (right), textile designer Manuel Canovas' arrangement of antique portraits, built around one large ribbon-hung painting, is a mixture of round frames with rectangular ones and small frames with large. On an adjacent wall, another group of prints is the very model of rectangular order and symmetry. ℂ In an ebonized secretary (above), a piece of late-nineteenth-century art furniture, designer Thomas Jayne propped old family photographs. He layered tiny frames in front of medium-size ones, then animated the small-scale exhibit with silver and copper bibelots and an art pottery vase blooming with dahlias.

Contemporary art as an accent piece is often daring, especially when it is dramatically staged. Artisan Tom Dixon's twisted metal chairs are a head-turning couple in their own right (opposite), but they are all the more compelling when shown on the cutout black spiral of a contemporary rug in this Manhattan apartment. ❦ In a living room that is a montage of pale ivory surfaces (above), a splendid cream-toned ceramic vessel by Richard De Vore commands center stage on a black iron table ~ itself a masterpiece by Diego Giacometti.

Janet Kardon, former director of the American Craft Museum in New York, and her husband filled their home with French Art Deco furnishings. To complement the exotic woods and sinuous shapes of their 1920s and 1930s furniture, they chose details that share the same visual richness, although not necessarily the same time period. Overlooking a Süe et Mare armchair in the bedroom is Robert Mapplethorpe's Calla Lily (opposite). The flower and chair possess similar curved shapes. ℂ In another mirroring of forms (right), a contemporary painting of concentric squares marries perfectly with an Art Deco sideboard with strongly linear side panels.

CHANCE ENCOUNTERS

COLLECTIONS formed by chance and good luck are always comforting. Like mashed potatoes and mother love, they sustain and nurture. This newly built Ozark Mountain retreat, home to a couple and their five children, is filled with friendly old objects that have come down from grandmothers and Lord-knows-where. "Browsing in antiques shops and junk stores has furnished the place," explains one of the owners.

In its simplicity of design, the pitched-roof house echoes the small, plain dogtrot cabins that generations of southern farmers built for their families. Architect Brian Stoner chose the architectural style because it is compatible with the hardscrabble pine-forest landscape. Like its prototype, the house was built to stave off the heat. Ten-foot ceilings and wooden fans keep the air circulating, and doors are aligned to let summer breezes waft through. A forty-foot porch blurs the demarcation between the house and the spectacular vistas that surround it.

Inside the weekend getaway, the owners turned the rooms into wondrous reflections of nature's landscape as well. On the living room walls, wildflowers abound and birds bob precariously on branches. They are all paper images: The creative wallcovering is composed entirely of prints from old Audubon and Redouté books discovered in junk shops and used bookstores, cut out, then placed close to one another in alternating bird and flower patterns. Against this gallery of charming paper ephemera, the owners hung larger bird prints in old gold frames.

More lucky finds from junk shops and family attics fill all the rooms. Vintage 1940s fruit-and-flower-printed dish towels hang over the big porcelain kitchen sink, and funky old lamps light the way in every room. Even the doors, amassed by Stoner, are a serendipitous collection ~ kitchen doors from a 1700s Vermont farmhouse and impressive mahogany front doors from the house of Franklin Pierce. With its parts gathered from so many places and so rich in history, the house, says Stoner, "is a kind of memory."

A slipcover cut from a floral fabric turns an easy chair into a captivating accent in the living room of this mountain cabin. The fabric, printed with camellias, the flowers that bloom in winter in the Deep South, seems cut from the same cloth as the Audubon and Redouté prints that blossom on all the walls.

Junk shops and old
furniture stores yielded
the vintage lamps
and comfortable chairs
that make the living
room a cozy place
(above). A screen door
leads to the "view
porch," which affords a
spectacular vista of
the wooded northwestern
Arkansas landscape.

A collection of children's
mugs, including
silver christening cups
and antique china
mugs emblazoned with
alphabets and nursery
rhymes, roosts on
an old country table
(opposite). A green 1940s
lamp is topped by a
cream silk shade frothed
with a ruffle.

CHAPTER 7

FORCE OF NATURE

INTRODUCING nature into a room literally injects the space with the force of life. Gardens, the woods, the seashore ~ they are all hunting grounds for beautiful objects worthy of display; these natural objects can help establish the personality of a design scheme as readily as any manmade accent ~ a clutch of white lilies in a glass beaker is a sophisticated yet simple finishing touch in a spare contemporary room, a bouquet of zinnias and Queen Anne's lace mirrors the charm of the American country kitchen it adorns. Mixed in with other accessories, nature's bounty introduces the spark of contrast: A grouping of cut-glass pieces looks livelier when one of them is filled with blooming red tulips. On a coffee table, a branch of coral set down next to a mother-of-pearl box and a marble bust makes the arrangement more captivating. The treasures of nature can be purchased, of course, but they don't have to be; they are all around, free for the taking.

A HARVEST OF RICHES

NO CATEGORY should be overlooked in harvesting nature's bounty. Floral possibilities include stem-cut flowers from the garden or florist, or even from the supermarket. Flowering plants and the lush greenery of non-flowering ones are lovely accents in any decor. A large orchid in a porcelain cachepot, metal urns filled with geraniums, a rose tree in a wooden tub, and trailing ivy in just about any container all possess as much drama as a large piece of sculpture when they are displayed on a table or the floor. The size of the container should always be appropriate to the volume of the plant or bouquet, and its color and finish should work well with the tones and textures of the petals and leaves.

Familiar fruits and vegetables from the green-grocer can become exotic jewels when formed into a decorative arrangement ~ a bowl of vivid oranges, a lineup of ripe green pears ~ or in combination with other objects, such as small boxes, baskets, silver, and pictures. As with flowers, containers count; the bowl, basket, or platter should be carefully chosen to enhance the color and texture of the produce on display.

The riches of the ocean ~ coral branches, sea-scrubbed stones, starfish, and shells ~ as well as terrestrial treasures such as rocks, fossils, and crystals are intriguing charms to bring home.

As with any other accents, natural details should be arranged with the guidelines of shape, color, texture, finish, and scale in mind. A vase of flowers may blend with a pale setting ~ all-white flowers in a cream-colored container, for example. Or a complete contrast might be more effective, perhaps bright blue delphiniums in a canary-yellow tapered vase. The rough texture of a chunk of crystal might be an ideal contrast to play against the smooth sheen of a sterling candlestick; a round picture frame propped on a console might be enhanced by the rococo curves of a conch shell placed beside it. There are as many possible combinations as there are exquisite details in nature.

In Mariette Himes Gomez's apartment in New York City, the severe geometry of a square urn is echoed by the shapes of the two frames on the wall above it. But the ivy in the urn is a buoyant contrast, a freeform, flowing bit of nature as graceful as the nudes in the drawings.

In a country setting, dried plants, twigs, and vines can become elegant ornaments. Overscale dried floral arrangements are very dramatic, all the more so when they are placed in large and unusual vessels. A case in point is the inspired display of nature on the wall of floral designer Spruce Roden's provincial-style dining room. The enormous oak grape harvester basket would have been adornment enough, but Roden heightened the effect by adding an armful of dried bittersweet berry branches, arranged so that they cascade over the container.

The owner of an eighteenth-century restoration embellished the sitting room mantel with a graceful arrangement of dried curly willow, vines, and greenery gathered from the woods around her house. To create a more dramatic effect, she positioned them so that they seem to grow off to one side, as if they were still rambling in the outdoors. The subdued colors of the plants and willow blend well with the stripped pine mantel and pale mottled plaster of the walls.

A bouquet of brilliantly colored flowers is arresting when it is displayed beside a painting, sculpture, or small ornament. In his country house, Charles Spada flanked a lyric landscape painting with equally poetic bouquets of lush hydrangeas in urn-shaped vases (opposite). ☾ A casual nosegay of late-summer flowers pokes out of a Stafford-shire jug (above left). The vivid tones of the pottery are a striking complement to the bright flowers. ☾ Designer Mary Douglas Drysdale picked a bunch of ranunculus in yellow and orange-red shades to echo the vivid surfaces of a bright yellow drawing room with orange silk curtains (above right). She set the bouquet on a tangerine lacquered coffee table and reined in a witty horse sculpture to stand beside it.

SOUTHWESTERN ELEMENTAL

FOSSILS, rocks and crystals, cactuses and animal horns, all natural jewels plucked from the landscape of the American Southwest, are the decorations Martha Hyer Wallis has gathered for her home in Santa Fe. With the help of architect Wayne Lloyd and interior designer Joyce Crawford, the actress has created a retreat that nurtures a rich life of writing, painting, and contemplation. The Spanish colonial adobe condominium is sparsely furnished, but it is filled with Wallis' extensive collection of Native American crafts, and nature is everywhere. Huge skylights and picture windows let in the sun, stars, and clouds. To bring the outdoors closer still, Wallis introduced the minerals and plants of the Santa Fe countryside into the rooms. Tall robust cactuses grow in giant metal vessels that rest on the stone floors. Rocks and fossils take their place among exquisite handcrafted objects. On the living room coffee table is a still life depicting the eccentric side of nature; a root bud and a fossilized tortoise shell share the space with a large piece of citrine. In the foyer, naturally shed antlers form a splendid chandelier. Flowering plants share the bedroom with Native American baskets and blankets. Under the dazzling New Mexico sun and the watchful protection of the Sangre de Cristo Mountains, these earth-born elements of nature are evocative reminders of a powerfully beautiful land and its nurturing serenity.

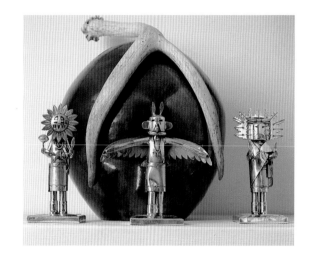

Green cactuses flourish in this adobe retreat as if they were growing in the desert beyond (opposite). The two-handled iron tub is a hefty vintage vessel whose large proportions suit the tall plant. The wall-hung pictograph of Blackfoot chieftains appears as if it were almost tethered to the plant. Fine examples of Native American silver from Santa Fe are displayed throughout the house (above).

Myriad elements of nature are integral to the design theme in Wallis' New Mexico home. In the living room (above), scores of logs are stacked in the niches cut into the adobe fireplace; their round ends create a pleasing pattern. The fireplace wall is crowned with a pair of antlers. In the foyer (opposite), rough beams left in their natural state form a grid over the skylight; the cloud-swept blue sky showing through is echoed in a Paul Kinslow painting at the far end of the room. Two chandeliers, hung side by side, were made from naturally shed deer antlers.

CHAPTER 8

ELEMENTS OF SURPRISE

A ROOM with a clever twist resides on the high ground of decorating. When an elegant women's fashion boutique in New York City opened a tearoom a few years ago, the main decoration was a wall of antique and art pottery teapots. The exhibit made design news and was widely copied. Teapots, of course, are not new; it was an unexpected presentation, which accorded each pot its own tiny gold-painted podium, that made all the attention-getting difference. ❡ Novel placement of accessories can relax a room ~ pictures that are hung unexpectedly high or low, for example, sound a casual note. Sometimes, an object is provocative when it shows up in a room where it is least expected. A bamboo ladder with boards slipped through the rungs to support stacks of books drew double takes when designers Stephen Sills and James Huniford placed it in a proper French salon. Climbing to nowhere, the slightly surrealist ladder chases stuffiness from the formal setting.

BREAKING THE RULES

USING A detail to create a note of surprise works best if it looks like a spontaneous gesture. Part of the charm of the ladder on the previous page is that it looks as if it had been unintentionally left behind in a grand salon. This unexpected note is a breath of fresh air that prevents an otherwise quite traditional interior from looking static or just too safe.

Objects that are not usually considered conventional accessories can make pleasingly offbeat details. Found objects, such as building finials and other architectural fragments, fall into this category. When the found object is taken out of its more humble context and put into a decorating scheme, the beauty of its shape and worn-paint finish becomes more apparent.

A stretch of the imagination can lead to other accessories that would work well as unexpected touches. Dollhouse miniatures are arresting on tabletops, especially the highly collectible Victorian and Edwardian examples. A plush dollhouse sofa perched on a side table is certainly not conventional, and the contrast of its tiny scale with the other objects around it is amusing and charming. Exquisitely crafted pieces of clothing can also make unusual accents. A group of colorful silk Chinese children's hats on stands is striking, if only because children's hats are not a usual design accessory.

Sheer contrast is a key element in creating an effective design surprise. In a grand room, a humble item, or one presented in a humble way, always turns heads. Most people display their children's artistic endeavors on the refrigerator. But one imaginative mother put her daughter's exuberant paintings in simple gilded frames and hung them in the rather dressy living room. The vivid colors in the artwork echoed the colors of the room's good English chintz fabrics ~ and the result was smashing.

Using an offbeat detail may require advance planning, but the preparation should never show. Any hint of contrivance would look strained, and then, of course, the surprise would be gone.

A painting or mirror would be the conventional choice to pair with a console table in a foyer. But in the apartment of Susie and Edward Elliott Elson, a raffia wall hanging, shaggy as a sheepdog, greets visitors instead. On the tabletop, the flat of green grass, which reiterates the fluffy texture of the raffia artwork, carries the offbeat surprise even further.

The customary way
to display art is framed
and centered on a
wall. But art that is
neither framed nor
precisely centered can
give a whole room
a casual turn. Avoiding
predictable placement,
Atlanta designer Nancy
Braithwaite arranged
framed prints at
chair rail level around
the perimeter of
a dining room. In this
smartly furnished
setting, the position of
the prints is the relaxed
equivalent of a well-
dressed man loosening
his tie, as well as
a unifier in a room
where each wall is
interrupted by a
doorway or windows.

*In an elegant
bathroom swathed in
striped wallpaper,
designers Ronald Mayne
and De Bare Saunders
deployed a beach
belle in a painting and
a queue of Egyptian
retainers on an urn, then
propped up a painting
of assorted fish and
a gilded sunburst mirror
(opposite). A stylized
wooden sculpture
stands guard next to
the pedestal sink
(left). Its exaggerated
height provides
still another surprise.*

MAINTAINING A
HIGH PROFILE

IT WAS JUST one of those things that clicked," says interior designer Sam Blount of the unusual placement he chose for his collection of antique silhouettes. Up high, just at cornice level, the pictures form a lively border that runs right around the living room of the Blount weekend getaway ~ a single decorative stroke that sets the room apart from a typical sweet and cozy country house interior.

"I have always been attracted to silhouettes," says the designer. "I find them historic and charming." Most of the genteel paper figures he has found are English, amassed by Blount over a ten-year period during trips abroad, and several were created by stellar practitioners of the art. Many of the pictures have the names and dates of the sitters on the back.

The charming severity of the little black and white silhouettes is a decided contrast to the house's creamy white walls and other furnishings, which are mostly pale-toned. From the time he and his wife bought the lilliputian 1825 house, Blount knew he wanted to use it to showcase his collection. The Early American architecture provided a perfect canvas, its beamed ceiling a decorative surface that lures the eye upward; the ploy might not have been nearly so successful had the ceilings been a blank white expanse or had they been been higher.

Determining the exact position of each picture was not easy, though. "It took hours and hours," recalls Blount. In the end, he alternated smaller pictures, usually heads caught in profile, with some of the larger ones showing several silhouetted figures in seated and standing poses. He played up the many pairs in the collection, positioning the larger ones on either side of a door or window and putting the tiny ones right next to each other. He avoided hanging anything else on the walls ~ "Other pictures would have conflicted," he says ~ to keep attention focused on the charming black-shadow cutouts.

Elegantly attired in tall hats and tea gowns, a parade of silhouetted figures hugs the ceiling of Sam Blount's country living room. Flanking the window is a matching pair showing two family groups. All other accessories in the room, including mirrors, shelves, and lamps, were chosen to be in appropriate scale with the silhouettes.

Blount placed other prints and accessories at ceiling height in the kitchen–dining room (opposite). A trio of vintage tins emblazoned with tartan patterns is lined up on the mantel. The designer hung three small silhouettes over the bed (above). The artworks are tiny, but their effect is considerable, thanks to judicious placement: Each of a pair of equestrian cutouts crowns a window, while a silhouette of profiled heads poses just beneath an antique circular mirror. Scaling the heights of the stair wall (right) is an antique American hobby horse. Horse brasses in a variety of designs are nailed to a strip of molding below.

DIRECTORY OF DESIGNERS AND ARCHITECTS

Jeffrey Bilhuber
Bilhuber Inc.
New York, New York

Sam Blount
Sam Blount, Inc.
New York, New York

Laura Bohn
Lembo Bohn Design
   Associates
New York, New York

Nancy Braithwaite
Nancy Braithwaite
   Interiors, Inc.
Atlanta, Georgia

Mario Buatta
Mario Buatta Inc.
New York, New York

Libby Cameron
Libby Cameron, LLC
Larchmont, New York

Steven Charlton
Goodman Charlton
Los Angeles, California

Jane Churchill
Jane Churchill Interiors
London, England

Eric Cohler
Eric D. W. Cohler, Inc.
New York, New York

Joyce Crawford
Joyce Crawford ASID
Phoenix, Arizona

Corey Daniels
Corey Daniels Antiques
Wells, Maine

Mary Douglas Drysdale
Drysdale Design
   Associates, Inc.
Washington, D.C.

Ann Dupuy
Holden & Dupuy
New Orleans, Louisiana

Jonathan S. Foster
Jonathan S. Foster Architects
New York, New York

Mariette Himes Gomez
Gomez Associates
New York, New York

Jeffrey Goodman
Goodman Charlton
Los Angeles, California

Kelly Greeson
Silver & Ziskind Architects
New York, New York

Albert Hadley
Parish-Hadley Associates, Inc.
New York, New York

Ann Holden
Holden & Dupuy
New Orleans, Louisiana

James Huniford
Stephen Sills Associates, Inc.
New York, New York

Irvine & Fleming, Inc.
New York, New York

Thomas Jayne
Thomas Jayne Studio
New York, New York

Joseph Lembo
Lembo Bohn Design
   Associates
New York, New York

Jorge Letelier
Letelier-Rock Design, Inc.
New York, New York

Robert K. Lewis
Robert K. Lewis
   Associates Inc.
New York, New York

Christian Liaigre
Paris, France

Wayne Lloyd
Lloyd and Tryk Architects
Phoenix, Arizona

Roger Lussier
Roger Lussier Inc.
Boston, Massachusetts

Gretchen Mann
Gretchen Mann Designs
Lyme, Connecticut

Ronald Mayne
Stingray Hornsby Antiques
   and Interiors
Watertown, Connecticut

David Mitchell
David H. Mitchell Interior
  Design
Washington, D.C.

Barbara Moller
Barbara Moller Interiors
Water Mill, New York

Charles Morris Mount
Silver & Ziskind Architects
New York, New York

Thomas O'Brien
Aero Ltd.
New York, New York

Peter Patout
Patout Antiques
New Orleans, Louisiana

Peter Pennoyer
Peter Pennoyer Architects PC
New York, New York

Carolyn Quartermaine
London, England

Frank Babb Randolph
Frank Babb Randolph Interior
  Design
Washington, D.C.

Katie Ridder
Peter Pennoyer Architects PC
New York, New York

Eve Robinson
Eve Robinson Associates Inc.
New York, New York

Spruce Roden
VSF
New York, New York

John Saladino
John F. Saladino, Inc.
New York, New York

Michael de Santis
Michael de Santis Design
New York, New York

De Bare Saunders
Stingray Hornsby Antiques
  and Interiors
Watertown, Connecticut

Barbara Scavullo
Barbara Scavullo Design
San Francisco, California

Stephen Sills
Stephen Sills Associates Inc.
New York, New York

Charles Spada
Charles Spada Interiors
Boston, Massachusetts

Michael Stanley
Putnam, Connecticut

Brian Stoner
New York, New York

Peter Wheeler
P. J. Wheeler Associates
Boston, Massachusetts

The room on page 1 was designed by Barbara Moller; page, 2, Albert Hadley; page 4, Mariette Himes Gomez; page 7, Corey Daniels; page 8, Thomas Jayne; page 11, Sam Blount; page 13, Jorge Letelier; page 14, Peter Patout; page 32, Ralph Lauren Home Collection; page 52, Eric Cohler; page 66, David Mitchell; page 86, Peter Patout; page 100, Ralph Lauren Home Collection; page 116, Thomas O'Brien; page 128, Stephen Sills and James Huniford; page 143, Frank Babb Randolph.

PHOTOGRAPHY CREDITS

1-2	Thibault Jeanson	54	Richard Felber	92	Lizzie Himmel
4	Thibault Jeanson	56-57	Thibault Jeanson	93	Jeff McNamara
7	Thibault Jeanson	58	Richard Felber	94-95	Dominique Vorillon
8	Andrew Garn	59	Christopher Simon	96	Antoine Bootz
11	Richard Felber		Sykes	98-99	Antoine Bootz
13	Jeff McNamara	60-61	Jacques Dirand	100	Thibault Jeanson
14	Thibault Jeanson	62	Peter Margonelli	102	Brian Whitney
16	Lizzie Himmel	64-65	Peter Margonelli	104	Lizzie Himmel
18-19	Lizzie Himmel	66	Walter Smalling	105	Antoine Bootz
20	Walter Smalling	68	Judith Watts	106	Andrew Garn
22-23	Walter Smalling	70	Mark Darley	107	Thibault Jeanson
24	Antoine Bootz	71	Jacques Dirand	108-111	Jacques Dirand
26-27	Antoine Bootz	72	Lizzie Himmel	112	Richard Felber
28	Peter Margonelli	73	Antoine Bootz (top)	114-115	Richard Felber
30-31	Peter Margonelli		Antoine Bootz (bottom)	116	Laura Resen
32	William Waldron	74	Antoine Bootz (top)	118	Thibault Jeanson
34	William Waldron		Jeff McNamara	120	Richard Felber
36	Gordon Beall		(bottom)	121	Lizzie Himmel
37	Michael Dunne	75	Antoine Bootz (top)	122	Antoine Bootz
38	Antoine Bootz		Antoine Bootz (bottom)	123	Antoine Bootz (top)
39	Dominique Vorillon	76	Walter Smalling		Dominique Vorillon
40	Antoine Bootz	77	Michael Dunne		(bottom)
41	Lizzie Himmel	78	Peter Margonelli	124-127	Lisl Dennis
42-43	Michael Dunne	79	Jacques Dirand	128	Antoine Bootz
44	Jacques Dirand	80	Dominique Vorillon	130	Jacques Dirand
45-46	Thibault Jeanson	81	William P. Steele	132	Langdon Clay
47	Jeff McNamara	82-85	Antoine Bootz	134-135	Kit Latham
48	Thibault Jeanson	86	Thibault Jeanson	136	Richard Felber
50-51	Thibault Jeanson	88	Jeff McNamara	138-139	Richard Felber
52	Jacques Dirand	90	William Waldron	143	Gordon Beall

ACKNOWLEDGMENTS

House Beautiful would like to thank the following homeowners: Rachel Blank, Jeffrey and Sharon Casdin, Robert Homma, Jerry and Susan Lauren, Catherine and Alessandro di Montezemolo, Richard and Joanne Stevens, Suzanne and Elliott West.

The photograph on page 41 was taken at the Kips Bay Boys and Girls Club Show House, New York, New York; page 66, the National Symphony Orchestra Showhouse, Washington, D.C.; page 70, the San Francisco Designer Showcase to benefit University High School, San Francisco, California; page 76, the Alexandria Community Y Decorator Showhouse, Alexandria, Virginia; page 81, the Kips Bay Boys and Girls Club Show House, New York, New York; page 128, the Royal Oak Foundation Showhouse, New York, New York; pages 134-135, the Litchfield County Designer Showhouse, Roxbury, Connecticut.